Master Your Emotions

How to Retrain Your Brain by Controlling Your Thoughts and Feelings. The Ultimate Guide to Upgrade Your Life, Improve Your Social Skills and Emotional Intelligence

By Dr. Kevin Carol Miyake

Table of Contents

Introduction

Life is an extremely tough journey. At times you get to the point where you ask yourself whether you will make it or not. Many people give up, while others postpone their plans just because things haven't gonged the right way.

The sad thing is that success and failure are all engraved in mind. The way you handle emotions and attitudes will determine whether you succeed or you fail. Just like anything else, anything you do takes practice and a lot of patience.

Through practice, you can learn to master your emotions. When you do this, you will be able to manage what is pleasant and what is unpleasant. Before you can get to this level, you need first to recognize the emotions and then label them. Give them a name and a size.

When you have time to master your emotions, you will find life being better and easier than it is at the moment. Make haste when choosing the right way to master emotions, because any slip and you will end up losing it.

We talk about mastering your emotions in this book. We look at the various emotions that you can have and how they impact your life. At the end of the book, you will understand what it means to be emotionally intelligent and why it is vital for you to master your emotions the right way.

Chapter 1: Quantum Physics and the Brain

Explaining how the human brain works may seem to have nothing to do with physics. However, several scientists have indicated that there is a strong correlation between quantum physics and consciousness.

The quantum theory is a component of physics that is used to describe how matter and energy behave in their natural state. This behavior is what is known as quantum physics. Correlation between this theory and the human mind is explained by a study done by Copenhagen, also known as the Copenhagen interpretation. This study shows that the quantum waves of a physical system decline when a person makes a conscious observation of it.

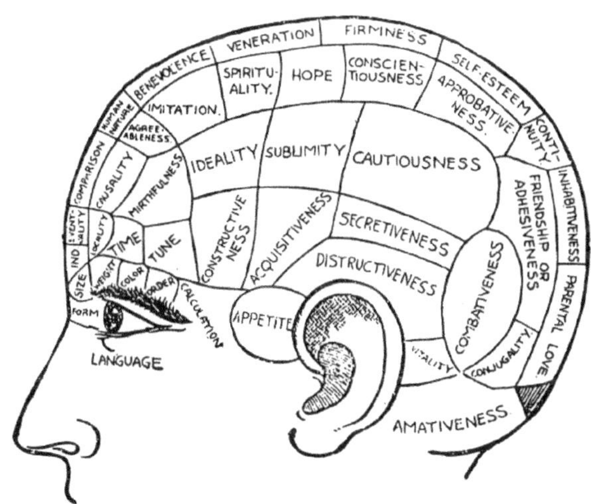

Image: The brain

A more advanced version of this theory was established in 1989 by Roger Penrose, who published a book on the law of physics and how this applies to the human mind. In his book, Roger explains how sophisticated the human brain is. He describes how the brain operates using computations that represent varying quantum states each time.

The idea to relate quantum physics with the brain originated from machine operation, especially the computer. Since the discovery of energy and matter, many people have been studying the world as a way of finding out how it works basing on the smallest unit of matter or the atom. Based on these studies, it is believed that anything in existence is energy and that every object comprises molecules which combine to generate energy. This is what led to the development of modern technological systems.

When it comes to quantum physics, everything begins with an idea. The entire universe operates on ideas. Research shows that everything that exists in the universe comprises of atoms. These atoms are created from energy, which arises from the human consciousness. This means that individuals create what is physical from the conscious, therefore translating what cannot be seen into what you can see.

The Quantum Universe

You can easily tap from this power by changing how your brain functions. Human beings are created with some level of intelligence, creativity, and desire for achievement at every stage of their lives. They are, therefore, capable of tapping into the quantum universe through the power of the conscious mind. You can easily do this by first selecting the kind of thoughts you wish to believe in. With these thoughts in your conscious mind, you can then connect your imagination to the quantum universe to create an idea in the physical.

The quantum universe requires that you utilize both the conscious and unconscious parts of your brain. Although it is not easy to achieve this, you can actually do it by:

- Identifying what you are good at
- Activating your conscious abilities like reasoning, imagination and intuition then using these to create a picture of your dream item or setup
- Translating this picture into your unconscious mind. As you continue to think about it, it becomes a belief or habit
- Continually doing number 2 and three until the picture you have in your mind becomes a reality

To achieve more in this process, find out those areas that you have a keen interest in and concentrate on building them. Identify your unique talent then build your life and career around this talent. Use this talent as your pillar and do not fear to share it with the world.

How Quantum Physics Relates with the Brain

The human brain works like a switchboard. It helps you to relate with both the unseen as well as the seen world. Most ideas come from connecting to the unconscious part of the brain since it is equipped with all the knowledge required to process information. Generally, the unconscious brain plays three essential roles. These are:

- Controlling the body's set of programs like attitudes, routines, and habits
- Operating the biochemical system of the body
- Creating a link between the mind and the quantum world of intelligence

Quantum physics also seeks to prove that the mind has a big part to play when dealing with reality. The theory indicates that things in the world can only become real when there is someone to act as an observer. It explains the universe as a space that contains uncountable super-positions.

A super-position is defined as the probability of a particle being at a given location during a specific time. These probabilities determine how the particles that make up the universe collapse to become a reality. According to scientists, all of this can only occur under observation. Therefore, the quantum theory concludes that the world and all the things in it can only be a reality when people make the necessary observations.

Since quantum physics explains the existence of everything found on earth, it covers the human brain also. Your thoughts, therefore, represent what you have chosen to observe. For example, if you start thinking about your family, relationship, career, or business, you have chosen to observe these aspects, which eventually translate into reality. Every instance of thinking translates the unseen into reality. Another example is when you peep through the window and start thinking about how beautiful it is outside. This automatically indicates that the kind of view you are looking at is full of beautiful things.

When it comes to quantum physics as related to how the brain works, it is clear that human beings determine greatly what becomes real in their lives. This is where affirmations come in.

Affirmation assists you in making the right choices about what becomes real in your world. Consciously selecting what you affirm about generates an observation and whatever you keep affirming about becomes a great reality. When you open your mind to great things, great things will likely happen around you. When you open your mind to nasty things, then these will likely become a reality within what you observe.

Affirmations are also emphasized trough the quantum zero effect, a major aspect of quantum physics. This concept demonstrates that you can sustain a particular state of the brain for a long time by creating rapid and more frequent observations about it. Quantum zero also indicates that those states observed for too long may become permanent in a person's life. This is because the mind is always changing all the time. If you decide to concentrate on a single thought, you create a force that is capable of sustaining the thought in your brain permanently.

Holding on to a thought permanently can totally change the state of your mind, resulting in new neural connections. When you keep focusing on positive thoughts, it becomes easy for you to create and sustain an ever-positive attitude. This, in turn, creates a positive reality and positive experiences. Generating positive affirmations needs concentration and determination. It is not easy to keep saying the same thing severally. There has been a lot of confirmation that persistent affirmation and positive thinking have a great impact on what happens in reality.

Image: thoughts have an impact on what happens in reality

Affirmations are crucial when there is a disconnection between the unconscious and conscious mind. In most cases, the unconscious mind gets to win because it is rich in knowledge. Here are a few guidelines that you can employ to ensure that you make the most out of the quantum nature of the brain:

- Understand that you are in charge of your world. Your thought patterns and actions determine your experiences in life. Whatever happens to you is largely dependent on your beliefs. It is therefore important that you determine the kind of beliefs that govern your life

- The unconscious mind can process an infinite number of things at a go. Therefore, you mustn't restrict the ideas and thoughts that come along

- Utilize neural linking, which involves connecting beliefs with emotions that are already present in your memory. Neural linking makes use of these connections to increase the effectiveness of your affirmations and beliefs. You can make use of this idea anywhere, anytime

- Develop some imprinting materials. These will serve as reminders that fashion your way of thinking. The materials can be in the form of audio recordings, pictures for those who are good at drawing, or writings

- Come up with a routine. Having a routine will train your brain's function. Routines that are more frequent always impact reality faster than those that occur at wide intervals. The best time to work on your thoughts is when you are a bit relaxed and not too busy. For instance, you may decide to do this every time you are half-asleep since at this point is when your conscious and unconscious minds are more alert. The ideal time recommended by scientists is very early in the morning when you wake up or very late in the evening as you go to bed.

The Use of Brain Waves

Just like physical waves, the brain also works using different types of waves. These waves determine your neural reconditioning capability and offer a basis upon which goals, aspirations, and beliefs are structured. They are produced through pulses generated from a wide array of neurons that communicate with each other. This communication is what becomes emotions, thoughts, and behaviors of an individual.

There are four common types of brain waves. These are:

- Alpha waves
- Theta waves
- Delta waves
- Beta waves

Alpha waves are the kind of waves that cause you to relax, acquire information through learning, and fall into mental sleep. They are responsible for meditation, intuition, and drowsiness. Alpha waves also facilitate access to the unconscious mind and provide the basis of the quantum aspect of consciousness.

Theta waves are essential for memory, and for acquiring new information and ideas. They are responsible for dreams and facilitate high levels of creativity. This kind of waves grant human beings access to the universe of intelligence and provoke most of the emotional experiences encountered on a daily basis. Theta waves are also responsible for promoting behavioral change. They offer a higher level of connection with the quantum aspect of physics.

The third type is the delta waves which are long. They are responsible for slow brain functions, and they do cause dream-free sleep. The delta wave causes a release of the human growth hormone that is responsible for cell development and regeneration. You can attain these waves at the awakened state of mind.

Lastly, beta waves are often at work when you are in your active state of consciousness. They are triggered by thoughts and action. Beta waves work faster than all the other types of waves. They are responsible for high attention and decision-making skills. They also trigger problem-solving capabilities.

These four waves are often distinguished through a sensor tool used on an individual's scalp. You experience each of them depending on your activity as well as your emotions. Slower waves occur when the mind is tired, while quicker ones occur in high energy. The speed of each wave is measured in cycles per second, commonly referred to as hertz.

Thinking Differently

Reality is not static. It keeps changing due to several factors. The quantum theory believes that a person's experience is highly subjective. The level of subjectivity varies among people depending on how strong they embrace a certain concept or idea. The more you embrace an idea, the more subjective you become. When an observer gets to connect with the universe, a lot of things happen. In this context, an observer represents any conscious being. Let us look at what happens in the universe for what you observe to become a reality:

- ***Your experience translates into an interactive process.*** Normally, observation is seen as a one-way task. However, when it comes to quantum physics, the setup is quite dynamic and becomes interactive as you engage your thoughts

- ***The experience is quite versatile.*** The truth is, the reality that quantum physics places before your eyes is one that flows freely and dynamically

- ***The experience is full of creativity.*** Positive affirmations and the desire to change always open up your mind to a high sense of creativity. This creativity is seen in the way you utilize your hopes, beliefs, intentions, and attention to customizing the reality around you

- ***Full of interesting encounters.*** Quantum physics makes the whole concept of the brain and how it works quite interesting. It brings in aspects such as matter, energy, the use of neurons and atoms which are absent in the basic explanation of the brain's functionality. The idea of observation is also new and brings a better dimension to the theory.

Quantum consciousness dictates how you view the world largely depends on your location as well. The array of things that you can think about, imagine, and create is always confined in the culture that surrounds you. This implies that your locality highly determines your level of quantum consciousness. The more you are aware of what constitutes your reality, the more dynamic you become in your perception towards the world around you.

Just like any three-dimensional object, space is also defined in terms of the length, width, and height. Since human beings operate within space, they are capable of moving within a single direction of time, and the rate of movement differs depending on several factors. The mind is a very dynamic part of the human body. It can trace memories of your entire life and even beyond. This is what explains the multiverse nature of the quantum field. Most of the things that happen in real life are a combination of several conceivable items. In some cases, the outcome of the conscious world is often uncertain.

The human mind can never exist as an independent object, and the limitations you face in life only indicate the type of observations you always make about life and the universe. Although you may not sense the universe daily, there are a whole lot of ideas and opportunities that you can gain from it. Quantum theory in itself is an outcome of the collective efforts by great minds. It explains the relationship between the particles that form the universe and gives you some insight into the operations of the human body and brain.

In the absence of an observer, particles in the brain behave as waves. Therefore, an observer must become part of the process of creating reality. The existence of an observer always impacts reality in a great way. It does not matter if this happens consciously or unconsciously.

Conscious observation is, however, essential if you need to change something about your life or reality. In this case, the observer customizes new intentions, thoughts, and ideas that can create a completely new reality. These changes impact the biochemical composition of the brain, causing a change in your physical body as well. Each time a thought flashes across the brain, some biochemicals are known as peptides flow into the blood, causing a change in emotions, feelings, and other forms of reactions. These reactions change the character of body cells, making it possible for you to express the changes in the physical state. The conclusion we make from all this is that if you want to change your reality, you must start by changing your way of thinking.

Chapter 2: Powerful Negative Thoughts

Everyone encounters some powerful negative thoughts once in a while. There are some that you can ignore, while others linger on however much you try. Negative thoughts that continue for long can pull you back or drain your general mood and health. They have a way of destroying your self-worth and can tamper with your potential to relate with others or complete some tasks.

The human mind is always engaged with thought. Negative thoughts always result in negative emotions, and these result in unpleasant actions. The mind always tends to focus on negative thoughts more than the positive ones. Learning how to identify these thoughts can help you to start controlling them. Some powerful negative thoughts may be challenging to overcome. However, you must always take note of these and ensure that you do not get fused with them.

Basically, negative thinking takes several different categories. Some of these include:

- ***Anger outpours.*** When you are maltreated by another person, you always end up having negative thoughts and feelings about the person. When you start seeing others negatively, it is likely that you will only think negatively about them.
- ***Overanalysis of issues.*** In the event that you are involved in critical decision making, it is crucial that you

assess all the available options. Some people tend to get obsessed about these options as they try to dictate the outcome. To avoid doing this, always have a deadline for making critical decisions. This ensures that you do not deviate from the positive aspect of the situation at hand.

- ***Negative reflection.*** This is also called negative rumination. Although there is a level of rumination that is healthy, especially if you want to head in the right direction of life, there is a level of reflection that may become harmful. This occurs at the point when reflection moments start generating negative thoughts and ideas. It mostly happens when you have spent a lot of time thinking about the same thing. The solution lies in switching to a different activity, idea, or environment as soon as you start deviating.

The Origin of Negative Thoughts

There are several reasons why negative thoughts occur. One major reason is the fear of the unknown. When you keep predicting the future based on the current reality, you may find yourself thinking negative things about what is bound to come. As you wonder whether the future will cause good fortune or harm, you may start predicting negative things, and this may result in negative thoughts.

Some people manage to maintain an optimistic view of what is to happen in the future. They then set goals based on their predictions and work towards achieving them. However, other people always find it difficult to remain positive in their thinking. Such people always think about failure or a looming calamity.

Another reason for negative thoughts is anxiety. When you get anxious about the present moment, you will remain worried about some simple things that do not even matter. For instance, you may leave your house in the morning and keep worrying as to whether you closed all the taps or if you switched off the lights. This, in turn, triggers some negative thoughts about what you may have forgotten to do.

Image: negative habits

The third trigger for negative emotions is a person's habits. There are people who spend most of their time thinking. Although thinking is healthy, it is vital to have a limit to what you spend time thinking about. If you make negative thinking a habit, you will always bear negative thought patterns. The more you concentrate on your thoughts, the more you will shift towards some thoughts that are not too good.

Another cause of negative thoughts is the occurrence of emotions. These always affect the mind and body. When a negative emotion occurs, it activates the brain to start thinking about it. If in any case, you encounter a negative thought that you cannot explain, it is likely that there is an underlying emotion that is causing such thoughts to arise. Any thoughts that arise as a result of emotion often act as a way of getting rid of the motion.

Your thinking capability can also determine whether you will remain positive or negative in your thoughts. The brain contains a good amount of energy that triggers conscious as well as unconscious thoughts. Unconscious thoughts are those that find their way to the brain without your knowledge. This is something that is beyond your control, and sometimes you may find that these thoughts are extremely negative. You can allow these thoughts to flow across your mind without focusing on them. This mostly occurs when you are idle

Examples of Negative Thoughts

Powerful negative thoughts make people see the wrong in everything that goes on around them. It always causes a decline in expectation as the person struggles with reality. When left unattended, these thoughts may result in long-term sadness, stress, or worry. Below are some fee examples of having negative thoughts.

- *Mind reading.* This is one major aspect of negative thinking where you keep thinking that you know the kind of thoughts others have towards you. For example, a person may ignore your calls, and instead of thinking of a valid reason why this could have happened, you start wondering whether you have wronged the person. This kind of thinking ruins relationships and may cause you to become a less social person.

- *Thoughts of guilt.* These thoughts arise when you have made a mistake and are in regret. Even when you are aware of the fact that you cannot erase past mistakes, you will always find yourself feeling guilty at a point. Not acknowledging your mistakes often leads to negative feelings and negative actions.

- *Low self-image.* Have you ever been doing something then all over sudden you started thinking that you are not good enough for the assignment? There are people who always think negative of themselves just because they do not trust their capabilities. When this happens, they always end up drowning in self-pity and spite. Such limiting thoughts always affect a person/s productivity and may lead to an inferiority complex.

- ***Fortune telling.*** This is also an example of negative thoughts where you always anticipate negative outcomes from situations. A fortune teller only thinks about the worst that can happen. This mentality hinders the person from appreciating any present moments that are full of bliss and fun. For instance, if you are scheduled to attend an interview, you may keep thinking that you are not going to succeed at it. This may make you nervous during the interview process, and eventually, the opportunity will bypass you. Fortune telling is a very bad character. It hinders you from attaining their goals in life and causes you to have less confidence in yourself. It also lowers your self-esteem.

- ***Blame.*** Blaming yourself and others is a result of negative thoughts. When you think less of yourself, you will always view yourself as a failure. This, in turn, affects your mood, and you may find it hard to let go of even the simplest mistakes. You will keep blaming others and yourself for things that are not your fault or responsibility. Doing this may result in destroyed relationships and business partnerships since it will be impossible for you to see any achievements made by those around you.

- ***Comparison.*** It is always easy to compare yourself to others. When everyone else seems to be living a good life based on their outlook and social media profiles, you may start harboring negative thoughts of defeat and failure in your mind. Doing make you become depressed.

How to Tame Negative Thoughts

Although you cannot eliminate negative thoughts completely, there are several ways you can use to control or tame these thoughts. Let us look at some of them:

1. **Meditation**

    Meditation is one of the most powerful tools used to rechanneled the mind in the right direction. It helps you to connect with the present moment as well as your current feelings. Meditation restores you back to the initial object of concentration. You can practice meditation each time your mind drifts towards thinking negatively. This technique does not eliminate the negative thought; it only redirects your focus away from the thought to ensure that your mood does not get affected.

2. **Changing Your Thought Pattern**

    Once you become aware of the occurrence of negative thoughts, you may try to review these into positive ones. You can start by trying to find out why such thoughts keep occurring then you can establish ways to deal with the source. You may also seek to tweak the narrative to include some positivity in it. For example, if you are worried about failing an exam, instead of thinking about it this way, you can assure yourself that you are going to try your best. This will help you to remain positive and composed during the entire examination period.

3. Have Positive Friends

One powerful secret of avoiding negative thoughts lies in surrounding yourself with positive thinkers. When struggling with negative thoughts, individuals who are not optimistic enough may make your mood worse since they will keep commenting negatively about your situation. If you are not able to influence the thinking of these people positively, then it is wide that you keep a distance.

When you surround yourself with positive thinkers, you may get assistance in overcoming your own negative thinking. Friends and family members who are ready to support you are better than people who have the same issue as yourself.

4. Be Grateful

Gratitude lists play several essential roles when it comes to remaining optimistic. Have a list of the things you are grateful for and refer to these each time a foul mood begins to arise. This will steer you into a habit of concentrating on the good side of things while ignoring the bad.

Besides writing good occurrences, you may also list some good attributes about yourself. These will go a long way in boosting your self-esteem. You can keep updating on these lists every day.

5. Affirmations

These are positive sentences and phrases about yourself or others. You can keep repeating these as an assurance that things will turn out positive. Affirmations also give you the opportunity to remain active throughout the day. They assist you to focus on the good things happening, and those that are about to happen.

6. Make Your Plan Flexible

Have an adjustable plan. It is true that things can get challenging at times, but when you have an adjustable plan, it is easy to fix yourself to accommodate any unexpected changes. When you start seeing challenges in your life and career negatively, you will start struggling in attaining your goals. Despite the negative challenges you face along the way, you should not allow them to deter your progress. Instead, always carve out a way out as you focus on achieving success.

7. Block Any Negative Forces from Outside

Do not allow the low energy of others to affect you. If you are a negative thinker, you must be careful that you do not allow yourself to sink into depression. One thing that you must avoid in particular is the negative energy possessed by others. You can either avoid such or just learn how to cope with their negativity.

If such people are family members, it becomes impossible for you to avoid them completely. Avoid engaging in any negative conversations started by such people, and in case they make negative comments about you, ignore them, and focus ahead.

8. Counter the thoughts with positive visualization

How you respond to the events taking place around you determines your future behaviors. Negative responses are always evident in your emotions and reactions if you do not work towards taming them. One way of programming how to respond to challenging situations is visualization.

The technique entails redirecting your thinking towards other possibilities of an occurrence instead of concentrating on the negative side of it. Instead of thinking about a negative possibility, channel your mind towards thinking of the many positive possibilities that can come about in the outcome.

Eliminating Negative Thoughts after an Affair

When your spouse or relation engages in an illicit affair, it is always normal to lose control of your emotions. Once this happens, it is possible that you will never see the person the same way you used to. Any thoughts that you have will mostly be negative. However, there are things that you can do to ensure that you do not get bound by these negative thoughts.

1. ***Do not blame yourself.*** You must come to a level of understanding that it is not your fault that your spouse cheated. Knowing that it was not your fault can help you keep off blaming yourself. If you do not this, you will be thinking of what you did not do right and if this may have triggered the affair. Blaming yourself may affect your daily life, and you may start struggling with your career and other important aspects of your life. No matter how bad the affair is, it is important that you do not see yourself as the cause.

2. ***Adjust your thoughts.*** Once you become aware of your partner's affair, your mind may start processing every detail of the occurrence. Doing this may get your thoughts beyond control, and you may start imagining things that are not true. Eventually, your self-esteem may be largely affected, and you may end up taking some regrettable actions. It is important that you erase your mind of any negative thoughts you may be harboring about the whole scenario. One way to do this is by meditation. You can also note down the negative thoughts that keep recurring. This will make the thoughts less important, and you will be able to overcome them without struggling.

3. ***Remain optimistic.*** When you get rid of the negative thoughts, try concentrating on positive ones as you gain more control of your brain. Identify the things you love doing and replay memories of these. Keep thinking about

those things that make you happy. This will leave very little room for negative thoughts. Doing this can take a while. You will need to be patient and consistent in your attempts. For instance, you can shift your focus on your children, job, or the good friends that you have.

4. ***Use spiritual resources.*** You may take advantage of some spiritual techniques to tame your mind and the thoughts thereof. For example, if you belong to a certain religious group, you can engage in some available opportunities that can help you to overcome what happened. In case you are a meditator, you can spend more time in meditation sessions to ensure that you get rid of all the negative thoughts and feelings.

5. ***Seek professional help.*** In case all the methods above are not working, you may consider getting help from a specialist. This is a person who will help you overcome every emotional and mental issue associated with the affair. The person will also advise on the necessary steps to take to ensure that you recover fully.

Chapter 3: Beliefs and How to Change Them

Beliefs refer to the many convictions and assumptions that people regard as truth. Every person always has a set of beliefs. People living within the same society or set up my share the same beliefs. Most beliefs originate from the experiences of life. They affect everything that goes on around a person's life.

Beliefs are crucial when defining a person's identity.

They also govern the knowledge systems and processes that define human beings. Beliefs play a major role in determining personality. They dictate behavior, reactions, and thoughts. They shape families, cultures, individuals, and society at large.

Image: different beliefs

Generally, beliefs can be divided into three distinct categories.

- Time-related beliefs
- Person specific beliefs
- Group-specific beliefs

Time-specific or universal kind of belief is those that are common in a wide array of people. These keep changing as time changes. They always dictate the kind of knowledge that people acquire within a given period. This kind of belief is often shared by people of different backgrounds, races, nationalities, and cultures. Some of them have been in existence for a long time and may not change any time soon. For example, for several decades, people believed that the sun revolved around the earth. It was until many years later that it was discovered that the opposite is true.

Individual or person, specific beliefs are always associated with an individual. They arise from a person's experiences in life, family values, and life history. These beliefs explain the uniqueness of each person and may be used to define personalities. Individual beliefs create a special world for every individual. They keep varying from one person to the other.

Cultural or group-specific beliefs are used to identify a set of people belonging to one group. These are different from universal beliefs because they are only limited to a specific number or culture of people. They govern cultures, religious groups, and small communities within society. Most cultural beliefs linger for longer periods and only a few changes with time. Such beliefs may be positive or negative.

Of the three, universal beliefs play a more important role in bringing people together. They ensure that people of different cultures and setups communicate effectively with each other. They also contribute a lot to the development of belief systems that govern the entire universe.

Beliefs always come about in two ways – through experience and through learning. Most of the beliefs people have were instilled in them from childhood. When a child is born, the environment and the family he is born to contributing greatly towards the kind of beliefs he will have as an adult. Friends and education systems also contribute some percentage of individual beliefs.

When you are young, it is easy for you to accept everything you are told, including that which is false. Every belief that you approve of gets stored as information within the subconscious mind. The mind cannot tell whether this belief is true or false. However, it triggers this belief to pilot the reactions and actions that one has towards some life experiences.

Impact on Life

Beliefs are vital for your day to day life. They affect a good number of aspects related to human life. Most of the things you do may be attributed to the kind of beliefs you have. Here are some specific roles played by beliefs in life:

- ***Beliefs affect behavior***

  Beliefs shape the reality of life by affecting how one behaves. For instance, if you believe that you are capable of handling a certain managerial position within an organization, you will always seek to apply for the position and work towards securing the job. This belief may also ensure that you remain confident throughout the interview process since you are confident about your abilities.

  Besides normal daily behaviors, beliefs may also impact a person's health practices. For instance, if you believe that an imbalanced diet causes diseases, you will always concentrate on eating healthy foods only. Also, if you believe that you are vulnerable to certain illnesses, you will tend to watch your diet more.

  The beliefs you have of yourself play a crucial role in determining the kind of person that you become. For instance, if you think that you are a bad person, you will keep thinking of ways to improve yourself. For instance, when you tell a child that he is doing a great thing by assisting others, he will increase the level at which he offers help to others.

- ***Affect the behavior of others***

  This can be a close family member, a friend, or a total stranger. For instance, you may gauge if a person is attractive or not just by talking to the person over the phone. A research carried out in the past indicated that women who sounded more attractive over the phone actually were more sociable and friendlier. Your beliefs may also influence the behavior of your partner. If you believe in your partner, he or she will give you more satisfaction in the relationship. People who are more satisfied with their relationships tend to experience fewer disagreements and fights. This is because believing in your partner instills the right level of confidence in them and eliminates the possibility of getting insecure.

- ***Beliefs affect health***

  Although several other factors often cause diseases and other health issues, research shows that your belief can determine the state of your health too. Studies show that a person who has positive beliefs, in general, is capable of living longer than one who has negative beliefs and thoughts. Optimistic individuals tend to suffer fewer heart problems than those who are pessimists.

  Negative beliefs may cause you to worry all the time, and this can result in stress-related complications. This stress can weaken the immune system and result in other complications.

People who always think highly of themselves release a substance that helps the body to increase immunity. This makes it easy for such people to fight diseases easily. When you fall ill, and you are given drugs, it is the belief that the drugs are going to work that helps you to overcome the disease.

- ***Beliefs prompt success***

Individuals who believe in having a lot of wealth often end up acquiring wealth. It is common for people to work hard but not get rich because of some belief against abundance. Most people attribute their wealth to the belief they had about money.

Belief also influences a person's ability in all areas of life. If you believe that you can achieve a certain goal, you will certainly achieve it. But if your belief is otherwise, then it becomes impossible to achieve the goal. For instance, if you believe in having good health, then you will work hard to ensure that you rarely become ill.

The way you work around your beliefs determines how much you achieve in life. For example, allowing your beliefs to influence your way of thinking comes with several positive outcomes. Doing this can help you keep any negative thoughts at bay so that you are not caught up in negative emotions and actions. You can also use your beliefs to determine how you plan your days so that you align your behavior to the goals you want to achieve. This will ensure that you move in the right direction to attain the success that you wish to have.

You may also organize your beliefs according to priority. There are those that are more powerful than others, and if you have a large list of them, you can prioritize those that are more important to those that seem less-powerful. For every belief system, what matters is the kind of beliefs that you maintain as a person. Your daily reality can be established as you continue restructuring your beliefs. When things become tough, you can make your beliefs work for you by asking yourself the following questions:

- What are some of the beliefs you have that are hindering you from moving beyond the challenge?
- Are there any positive beliefs that you need to put more focus on to ensure you succeed in your efforts to overcome the challenge?
- Which beliefs do you need to keep to ensure that you sustain your growth once you overcome?

Responding to this question ensures that you continue living a fulfilled life once you have attained your dreams.

How to Change Your Beliefs

Change always occurs when a person makes the decision to adjust accordingly. Changing your beliefs starts with acknowledging those beliefs that are of no use to you. If you want to live a fulfilled life, you must always spend time analyzing your beliefs and improving on them accordingly.

Changing your beliefs involves identifying false ones and replacing them with those that are true. There are several theories and methods that you can use to rewire your belief system. Applying these to your life often involves very simple steps that need to be repeated severally. These steps include:

1. ***Identify a belief that needs to change.*** You can do this by analyzing your list of beliefs. Then pointing out those that have been working against you. For instance, you may be holding a general belief that no one should be trusted. This belief might have made you stop believing in other people, including the ones you are dating. Due to this, you may have lost so many relationships for nothing, and maybe, you have been regretting over the same. If this is the case, you can then list this belief among the ones you need to either adjust or eliminate completely. When doing this, however, you must ensure that indeed, the belief is false and what happened was not a reality.

2. ***Replace the beliefs on your list with proven ones.*** For example, if you had distrust as your belief, you can start telling yourself that people are trustworthy and honest. Create a belief based on your past experience as well as the knowledge you would have gathered from others. Train your heart and mind to believe in the new

facts so that you do not continue being limited by the old, false concepts.

3. ***Continue to remind yourself of the new beliefs.*** This is important if you have spent a long time believing the ideas that you just got rid of. Once you replace these, it is necessary that you keep exercising your new beliefs as well so that you do not get to go back to the old ones. Most people do this every early morning as they wake up, during the day and in the evening just before they get to bed. You can work out a routine that suits you, so long it is one that will ensure that you master the new belief. The more you remind yourself, the faster it sticks in your subconscious mind. Eventually, you will start noticing a change in your actions, feelings, and thoughts in response to the new belief changes.

4. ***Create a new experience.*** Apply the belief in your daily life to see how it will affect you and those around you. For instance, since you trust people more now, you can start exhibiting more confidence in others and see how this will impact your relationships with them.

Changing Belief Systems in Business

By definition, a belief system is a collection of beliefs and ideas that one uses to create meaning from the world. In ancient times, individuals used to do this by use of supernatural occurrences. Things have changed now, and most people believe that scientific evidence is the best way to make sense from the world. One researcher is known as Karl Popper, for instance, sought to describe the difference between scientific and religious beliefs. He stated that religion represented a closed system while science represented an open system. By this, he meant that religion monopolizes the truth because it does not allow for revision of the beliefs involved. On the other hand, scientific beliefs are always changed based on new research findings and criticism from the world.

Belief systems always drive behavior. They work in conjunction with things like genetics, habits, and personality to drive the decisions someone makes. They also define how you communicate with others and how you respond to the challenges and situations in your surroundings. Belief systems create an environment for human beings to thrive, and individuals accumulate them as they continue growing and living. Beliefs also interact with each other and work together to form some sort of system that acts as a force in life.

The elements of each belief system are always fashioned in a way that ensures you achieve your goals in life. In a nutshell, the system comprises the following characteristics.

- Belief elements that work as a set
- The beliefs are connected one to another
- They work together to accomplish a certain mission

The belief system can also be expanded to consist of a person's assumptions, opinions, and values.

Since beliefs are always interconnected, changing one belief always affects the entire system. If the belief you change is a major one, adverse effects will be experienced. You may need to reset the entire list to ensure that you build one that is more effective. Most belief systems also evolve on their own as time goes by to ensure the overall survival of mankind.

When it comes to the business world, beliefs always affect a person's negotiation, decision making, and communication skills, amongst others. They determine how a person achieves certain ranks in organizational and leadership hierarchies. They also help you to maintain a healthy mental status through fostering ways that help reduce stress and anxiety. This depicts belief systems as a set of sub-components that ensure that every aspect of your life works according to expectation.

Before we look at how to change your belief systems for the workplace or business, first let us detail the key elements that define the system. These are:

- ***Homeostasis*** – this indicates that system elements have a uniqueness that does not disrupt the stability of the system when changed. The beliefs always work towards attaining a certain level of equilibrium. This ensures that the system remains stable even when you implement some changes to its components.

- ***Autopoiesis*** – belief systems have a capability for self-maintenance and reproduction. This means that even if you do not change anything in the system, there will still be some changes based on other factors that are beyond your control. The more a system exists, the more complex it becomes.

- ***Self-regulation*** – the system adjusts itself based on some external factors and conditions. These factors arise from the environment in which the beliefs are exercised. This aspect ensures that the system works despite the circumstances in the surrounding. When you get access to new beliefs and ideas, the system automatically readjusts itself and assumes a different setup altogether.

This means that you should not get worried whenever you feel at a loss of your beliefs, especially when undergoing a tough time. Such an experience only means that your belief system is working to restructure itself depending on what you have been exposed to. You should, however, get worried if this goes on for prolonged periods as this may indicate that something is wrong. At this point, you may need to seek professional guidance and assistance to identify the problem. This will help you reconstruct your actions, thoughts, and decisions better by exposing yourself to better things, better ideas, and a better environment that is suitable for your belief systems.

When seeking to change your business belief systems, you need to ask yourself some critical questions. Some of these questions include:

- What are some of your primary beliefs and among these, which are the ones that seem questionable? What are the reasons for questioning them?
- What are some of the beliefs you have encountered in the recent past that need to be incorporated in your belief system? How did you establish the validity of these beliefs?
- Which of your old beliefs seem to be hindering you from accelerating towards your goals?
- Which environments do you need to operate in to help you put the new beliefs in practice?
- What do you want to become in the future, and does your current belief system ensure that you attain this?

Choosing the right environment for yourself ensures that you do not strain your belief system. Changing your system automatically means that you need to change your environment as well. For instance, if you decide to venture into a completely different career field, you may need to change your department or organization totally.

Remember, the basis of changing your belief system lies in how you perceive it. If you regard your system too high, you will not see the need to change it. However, if you get exposed to beliefs and thoughts that are contrary to your current system, you will start seeing the need for revising your current beliefs accordingly. Sometimes it will take a long time for you to implement a new belief, sometimes not.

At other times, you may notice new beliefs very quickly, and this means that you may need to incorporate them into your system faster as well. This mostly happens when you get exposed to a new environment or community. You must be careful that these sudden changes do not affect your emotional stability or sense of self-awareness. Most individuals experience a mix of emotions such as frustration, confusion, anger, and shock since the new change was not anticipated.

The most impactful change in your belief system is that which affects your core beliefs. These are beliefs that are quite instrumental in determining e kind of person you are known to be. Changing these beliefs often means changing the very essence of your existence. For instance, when you get into a new culture, you may suffer from a strong culture shock since most of the things than by those who belong to the new culture contradict what you believe in.

When this happens, you may start to develop some negative emotions. This, however, does not mean that something is wrong. Therefore, you should not focus all your attention on these negative feelings since they will keep fading as you adjust to the new environment. This is how growth takes place.

Chapter 4: Factors Affecting Emotions

Sometimes, emotions arise for no apparent reason. Sometimes, it is due to some internal or external factors. The emotional state of a person can be very dynamic, especially if the person has not learned how to control his or her feelings.

One great influence for your emotions is *perception*. How you perceive things or situations greatly affects the chemical changes that take place in your body. For example, if you view an occasion as a problem for you, you will experience either hatred or fear towards the occasion. If you intend to speak or address people on such an occasion, you will probably experience anxiety during the session.

 If you perceive the same occasion positively, you will appear more relaxed. You will also feel some excitement as the day of the occasion approaches. These are two different kinds of emotions arising from the same occurrence. That means that how you view life and the events in it determines how your emotions behave.

Image: perception can be right or wrong

The way you perceive others also determines how you interact with them. For instance, when you have a negative perception towards others, you may find that the responses you give them are somewhat hostile even if the question asked was a simple one. If you have a positive perception towards others, your engagement with them will be a fulfilling one, and you will leave them happy. It is, therefore, important that you control your perception to ensure that you appear emotionally intelligent.

Your *mental health* can also affect your emotions. Stress and the lack of stress always manifest physically as well as emotionally. Physical manifestations of stress may include muscle aches and general body pain. Emotional signs are things like anger, sadness, and anxiety. Your stress levels greatly affect your mood. It is therefore crucial that you learn how to manage your stress by identifying the source of the stress and dealing with it appropriately.

Lack of sleep impacts your general mood during the day. It is always enjoyed staying up late, especially when doing something that is fun. However, doing this continuously can interfere with the functional ability of your body. You may start feeling moody all the time, and this may result in serious health conditions like stroke and heart problems. To relieve yourself from such occurrences, always ensure that you get enough sleep. The recommended hours of sleep for every individual is between seven and nine hours. If you are an early riser, it is important that you sleep early enough.

Hormones can also cause emotions to fluctuate significantly. For example, women whose bodies have low levels of estrogen hormone may notice drastic changes in their emotions. Testosterone hormone levels may also cause a mood problem in men. Tests can be carried out to determine if hormones are responsible for the mood changes experienced by a person.

Some foods may be responsible for mood fluctuations as well. For instance, chocolate causes a trigger in sugar levels and endorphins. This results in a feeling of pleasantness and excitement.

Each emotion always comprises of two components – a bodily component and a mental component. These two also affect a person's mood and feelings differently. The mental component of emotions is characterized by:

- The ability to differentiate and choose between pain and pleasure
- The tendency to engage inactivity
- Memory thought, and perception of an individual. These three aspects define the social, mental, and material interests of human beings
- Ability to differentiate between muscular and organic sensations

The bodily component of emotions, on the other hand, determines:

- Any changes in the body's internal organs as a result of emotional changes
- Movement of body muscles

The mental component is what comprises an emotional experience while the bodily component is what is known as emotional expression. Basically, emotion is often triggered by the imagination, thought, or perception of a particular circumstance. It is not triggered by a single thing or event but a collection of mental activities.

External occurrences cause different kinds of emotions. For instance, seeing a leopard always triggers fear of getting harmed or losing a life. However, seeing the same leopard in a cage will not trigger the emotion of fear.

Every emotion is a response to a situation. It can be pleasant or painful, depending on your perception of the situation.

Emotions and the Environment

Your surrounding greatly determines the kind of emotions you generate. A home or place that is adorned with bright, shiny colors will always make you happy and at ease. The surrounding alone will improve your mood greatly. However, places like call centers or chat rooms with dull walls, and nothing colorful in place will always create a gloomy environment. There is nothing exciting about such environments. This explains why most workplaces do not get too many decorations.

Workplaces are not placing of excitement but places of serious business. However, your overall mood always affects how you respond to certain situations. For instance, if you are in a gloomy environment and a challenging issue arises, your response may not be quite good, especially if you have had quite a long day. If you have been confined in such an environment for long hours, you may feel frustrated by the new issue that has arisen and may end up getting angry at everyone.

Negative emotions always have a negative effect on your ability to perform your duties. Some environments can create a negative mood, and as a result, you may start developing negative emotions out of nowhere.

Most interior designers understand the place of colors in determining the mood in the room. For instance, most people use white and gray in the workroom, yet research shows that individuals who work in rooms painted in these colors tend to become less active and productive.

One example of individuals who get overwhelmed with the work environment is call center representatives. They are always faced with an expectation that some cannot meet. Customers always expect them to remain confident and joyful at all times, regardless of how their day has been. However, this sometimes becomes impossible, and their emotions may run beyond control.

The color of the room also affects the mood of those in the room. You should thus understand which colors inspire a positive environment and which ones create a more productive atmosphere. Some of the colors associated with a great mood include:

- ***Blue*** – this is a great color for you if you wish to experience calm. The blue color is also known as a remedy for high blood pressure. It also stimulates the mind to think positively and causes individuals to become more productive. When balanced with other colors like yellow, it can also create a good setup for creative thinking, which is a catalyst for circumstances that require adequate problem-solving skills.

- ***Red*** – red is a very powerful stimulant. However, it should be used in moderation. Red is a good color for settings that promote serious physical activity. In environments that need some calm, you should use red sparingly since the color is known to stir energy and action.

- ***Green*** – the green color also creates a calm environment. One great thing with green color is that it is found freely in nature. That is why people who need to relax spend most of their time outdoors. Green also acts as a source of balance for other colors, and it triggers productivity.

Besides colors, the lighting of an environment may also trigger negative or positive emotions. For instance, blue lights often promote a sense of creativity in the workplace and create a calm environment in the home. Studies show that being exposed to blue lighting improves performance significantly. Natural light also plays a big role in the home or work environment. It causes people to relax more, giving them better control of their emotions.

To summarize this, let us look at a few ways through which the environment affects individual emotions.

- Most of the environmental factors that a person cannot control like noise and heat always act as stressors. These often trigger negative emotions

- The setup of a room can enhance communication and interaction. This, in turn, results in lower palpitations and a significantly reduced blood pressure. Socializing also improves your general mood and excites the body at a level that is similar to engaging in physical exercise.

- Natural environments always act as stress relievers. Getting into contact with nature, lowers anger, fear, and anxiety levels by a good percentage.

- The color of your room can impact how you feel about yourself, the environment, and others. Research shows that individuals who spend time in a place with green walls concentrate more than those who spend in a room that has red walls. When used generously, red color always causes anxiety.

- The scent of a place can also enhance or destroy one's mood. For example, the smell of fresh grass or leaves causes happiness, while the smell of pine leaves causes the mind to relax.

- Natural or artificial light that is nature-related always alleviates depression symptoms. It also facilitates sound sleep and makes you less agitated

Emotions and Behavior

There are emotions that cause people to react in a certain way, and this affects how a person thinks. This is always helpful when danger is involved. Sometimes, things happen, and there is no time to think before acting, but there are some emotions that trigger a lot of thinking. For example, if you encounter a person that is undergoing a challenge, the feeling of sympathy or sorrow may cause you to start thinking about how you will assist the person.

Negative emotions mostly lead to negative thoughts, while positive emotions often lead to positive thoughts. That is why it is essential that you change your way of thinking. For example, if you sit an exam and fail it, you may start thinking that you will never pass the exam, and this assumption may cause you to stop working hard. When this happens, you should analyze the situation to understand better why you failed in the first place. This will help you to improve on the areas that need development so that you can perform better next time.

Most emotions often show in the person's face or actions. A good example is when you are angry. You will either raise your voice at others or make somebody's movements that suggest your agitation. The anger may also show on your face as frowns or clenched teeth. Some of these actions are predictable, while others occur without expectation.

Actions always indicate an expression of feelings. That is why it is not advisable to suppress your feelings, even if they are negative. Trying to suppress your feelings can cause mental and physical problems.

When it comes to behavior, emotions also affect the way a person makes decisions. Negative emotions always trigger negative decisions since they make people feel like they have very limited options available. When you are excited, you are always bound to make unrealistic decisions that are regrettable. That is why it's advisable that you do not make decisions when highly agitated or highly excited.

As for the workplace, emotions can impact the motivation, personality, and temperament of a person.

They cloud a person's sense of perception and judgment. Emotions also play a major role in determining how you react to the stimuli that occur in your environment. When you are exposed to negative emotions for a long time, you may develop some sicknesses such as ulcers and heart problems. This also applies to stressful environments at work and at home. Generally having a bad mood always reduces the performance of individuals since this makes employees make poor decisions that may affect the company's overall performance.

On the other hand, a positive wave of emotions boosts problem-solving and creativity skills of employees. As earlier stated, emotions are caused by a chemical balance in the brain. This chemical balance always determines an individual's mood and energy level. It also enhances or diminishes one's thinking and judgment capabilities. Individuals must, therefore, seek to identify how their emotional state affects their behavior as a way of improving how they interact with others and respond to situations. Positive emotions always lead to satisfaction; therefore, it is always important to ensure that your emotions are adequately balanced.

Chapter 5: Mind Control

Also known as thought reform, mental control, coercive control anymore, this is the use of different techniques to change the way you think. It is all about making sure you change the way you think about someone or something regarding yourself.

Mind control is seen as a system of influences that will disrupt your very core, the level of your identity (preferences, values, beliefs, decisions, relationships, and behaviors. The result is you create a new identity or a new personality.

Image: your mind is an empty canvas

You can use mind control in various situations.

Why does Mind Control work?

Mind control works because the mind is susceptible. Everyone is susceptible and receptive to manipulation techniques. Mind control for you works because the mind can be manipulated so that it thinks something different.

Unlike the other type of mind control technique that you are under another person's spell, this time it is you who us aware that you are doing things to change the way you think and feel. You can control various variables such as the time as well as the environment in which you work. You try to repress previous attitudes and behaviors while installing new attitudes and behaviors.

What Affects the Effectiveness of a Mind control Techniques?

For you to enjoy the benefits that come with mind control techniques, you need to look at various aspects that affect the outcome of the process. These include:

- The types of techniques that you use to achieve mind control.
- The number of techniques that you apply to your mind.
- How often you expose the different techniques to your mind.
- How long you are exposed to different techniques.
- The kind of support that you get from friends and family.

If you feel that you are out of control and you are a constant slave of your emotions and thoughts, you need to change this situation. Being able to control your mind is a huge pillar of wellbeing and overall health.

When it comes to enjoying good health, very few people have the guts to look above the neck; they mostly look at the rest of the body.

They ignore the emotional health and mental health – when, in reality, everything is closely connected.

Good physical health without a healthy mind doesn't translate into true health. This is because they are all connected and communicate with each other. The mind has a huge impact on the body as well as physical health.

Therefore, when you master your mind and thoughts is a vital factor in overall health and wellbeing, and you cannot ignore it at all. You need to take care of the mind because the brain depends on nutrition for it to function at its optimum.

Situations when Your Mind Controls Your Life

The mind is such a funny thing – on one part it is very awesome while on the other it can make you ruthless.

At times, the mind is scared and cautious. Well, this is its job, and it helps us survive. It helps you cross roads safely and avoid situations that can put you at risk of injury.

But your mind has a system of its own, and it uses this system to boss you around the way it wants.

The tendency of the mind to want to control you is so strong that you usually don't realize it when it has taken up control over you.

The bad news is that there is no book that will teach you how you change the mind; the good news is that you can do it by yourself.

Let us look at the times when the mind tries to steal the show:

1. *Ignoring Your Natural Inclination*

The mind isn't wise; it is just naturally smart. It is just all about looking at facts and making various decisions, telling you what next to do depending on the odds.

For instance, you decide to visit a friend that you haven't seen for a few weeks, but your mind tells you that the person isn't home, so you lie back on the couch and start watching a movie.

Have you ever followed what the mind wants and then looked back later to find out that things would have worked out differently if you would have gone with your intuition?

What about the decisions that regard your life? The most logical explanation for choosing the career that you are in at the moment is that experts guided you to make the perfect choice, but when you look back and then consider what you would have ended up with, you might regret later.

This is why you always ignore the little voice that tells you to be a teacher, and then you choose a job in banking because statistics show that there are a lot of opportunities in the sector.

Remember that just because your brain tells you that you are good at something, it doesn't mean that you have to go ahead with it.

2. *You Can't say No*

Do you have issues with saying no to something that someone wants from you?

You might not see it as a huge problem, but when you are a pleaser, you will end up spending the whole of your life pleasing other people and satisfying their whims while your needs take the backseat.

When you are a pleaser, you feel like there are rules that compel you to do something even if you don't want to do it. You feel that you have to be the best friend; you have to be the best lover and more.

This is all about your mind – you have no capacity to say no because you want to be liked and the mind thinks that everything that other people want from you is more important than what you need.

You need to remember that it is your right to do what you want; it will benefit everyone when you do.

3. *When You Are Constantly Looking for Approval*

People love the internet and emails, and they love reading comments on blogs. This is an awesome world that we live in, but it makes you live off balance the way that you use it.

It is not all like you are working or doing something so awesome online; you are constantly looking for approval on the social platforms.

The need for approval runs deep – it is not only a natural trait of the mind, but it is also entrenched in by the education system. The more likes you get on integral might be more important than what you will get at work from your colleagues.

But this fact is so dangerous; this is because it keeps you living in fantasy land and trains you to be so worried when people tend to disagree with you on any topic.

This is like brain candy – the more you take in, the more you desire.

Do you need to give it all up? No – what you need to do is to set limits so that you keep everything in check.

4. Resisting Change

Change is inevitable – you need to try and change what you think, depending on the prevailing situation. However, at times, your mind decides that things shouldn't be the way they need to be, and it resists anything new that you introduce to it.

The mind is worried that you will want to make that giant leap of your own and it will tell you not to do anything.

We all have the capacity to make things better, opt to leave them as they are. This is why you need to take part in activities that will introduce you to new things that will take you to new heights. The resistance to change is all about you understanding what you want and taking charge of your life.

5. *Trying to Control Someone else*

Have you ever felt that you know someone else better than they do and you need to get them to do things in your way? Well, the mind will tell you how you need to intervene to make things better for the other person, but the truth is that you shouldn't. The mind usually thinks that it knows better than what you need to know, but for sure, it doesn't.

When you try to control other people, whether in small or in big matters is not only disrespectful and annoying, but it also stops the flow of life. When this happens, you miss out on a lot of things.

If someone has ever tried to control you, then you know what it entails and how annoying it can become.

The Benefits of Controlling Your Mind

Before you can put in any work, it is vital that you understand the various benefits that come with learning to control your mind. Let us look at the few benefits:

You lead a Disciplined Life

When you plan out your day the right way and then work with the plan, you will be able to do all the work that you have allocated to you. This will be amazing for you.

Lead a Life Filled with Positivity

When you learn to control your life, your mind will be full of positivity, and you will learn to open new doors of opportunity.

Determination

When you chase the different goals of your life, you will fail if you lack determination. Failure doesn't make you give up on goals. When you learn to control your mind, you will get to learn from failure, and you will, therefore, turn your failings into success because you won't repeat previous mistakes.

You Are in Control

It feels good to be in control at all times. Whenever you feel negative thoughts taking over your life, you will trash them and then give yourself some rules that you will follow.

Enjoy a Stress-Free Life

When your soul and mind are filled with positivity, you won't have any room for stress to destroy your peace. You can live a life free of stress.

How to Change Your Thoughts and Transform Your Life

The good thing about all this is that the mind can be controllable. Let us look at the various tips that you can use to change the way you feel or the way you do things.

Use Positive Affirmations

Well, you know too well that affirmations aren't always positive, they can also be negative.

The sad thing is that many people only use negative affirmations when talking to themselves or when they plan to do something. For instance, when faced with a huge task, many people will first make negative affirmations that will then become their truth.

Affirmations have an impact on the decisions that the brain makes, which is the reason why you need to have positive ones that will make you go for good things.

Positive affirmations work like mantras; they come with a spiritual and sacred force about them that will make you stronger. Avoid negative thoughts such as "I can't," "I might" and focus on affirmations such as "I should', "I can," and more.

Remember that the brain is always adapting to thought patterns that you pick up, and it then directs your organs to react the right way.

Know When to Stop

You might do something, but you won't do all the things all the time. If you make a mistake, you need to know the right time to stop when you make a mistake. Stop cursing yourself over what you would have done differently at any time.

This shouldn't mean you don't need to look into your past mistakes so that you can plan your future intelligently; instead, you need to know what to take up from your past and what not to take up.

Count Your Joys

Many times, we focus on our misgivings and then forget that we have had good times before. Many people look at their joys and blessings for granted, and then they start complaining about what they lack and what they missed.

They think of a situation that could be better by now and forget the ones that might have turned out worse than they already are.

When you learn to appreciate something, you make it possible to unlock the joy of life. It makes you see what you have to be enough and to be more than enough. You will be able to turn denial into acceptance, confusion into clarity, and chaos into order. It can even turn a stranger into that friend that you always wanted.

Instead of complaining over what you don't have, it would be better to enjoy and appreciate what you already got. If you have achieved some success so far, you need to aspire and enjoy what you have done so far instead of feeling sad that you haven't achieved what you dreamt about.

Savor the Thrill of Your Achievement

It is one thing for you to achieve your goals, and it is another thing for you to enjoy it when you have achieved it.

So, you need to aim for something, and then once you achieve what you aimed for, you enjoy it so that you go to the next.

Hold Your Head High

Many people always tend to feel low when they are faced s by demoralizing conditions. They feel low, and this shows in the way that they talk and walk. If you tell your brain that you are feeling low, then it will communicate to your organs, and they will act according to the communication – you will feel more miserable.

On the other hand, if you train your brain to read only the positive vibes even in trouble, you will be able to lift your spirits, and then your body will react the same way. This is the best way to beat depression when things are going wrong.

Seek Happiness in the Present Time

Don't associate your happiness with the future; rather, you need to be happy in the present. When you postpone your happiness to the unsure future, you will end up living in sorrow all the time. The time for you to be happy is now because yesterday is gone.

Master Your Emotions

You need to always be a master rather than a slave to your moods. You need to be a ruler of your happiness kingdom. Try and make sure other circumstances and people don't determine your moods.

Many people tend to depend on material possessions to be happy, try, and get your happiness from within yourself regardless of the situation.

For instance, if you have been ditched by your girlfriend, don't allow the heart to be a slave to their emotions. If the person has decided to be happy without your presence, then you also can do the same.

Meditate Daily

Meditation helps you to connect with your inner self in ways that you cannot imagine. Try and find the best meditation approach that will help you to manage your inner feelings at all times.

Talk to a meditation expert and identify the best method that you can use to meditate on a daily basis. Get the right time to meditate, whether early in the morning or late at night so that you can meditate the right way.

Chapter 6: Overcoming Fear

Fear is the feeling that you encounter when you think about a person or something that might harm you. When you experience fear, you get the urge to get away or avoid the threat.

As an emotion, fear is evoked in you when there is a concrete threat to your environment. For instance, the mere thought of a car that is fast approaching you or a spider that crawls on your arm can lead to the feeling of fear in you.

Image: fear of the future

Fear is characterized by things that haven't happened yet – it is about what will happen in the future.

There are so many threats that can evoke fear in you; these include:

- The treat of getting harmed.
- Loss of financial or material possessions.
- Being afraid to say the wrong thing.

- Loss of friendship or closeness.
- Hurting other people.
- Fear of embarrassment.
- Fear of loneliness.
- Fear of disgust.

Usually, fear is evoked when you get into a situation that will evoke any of the emotions that have been described before.

When you experience fear, you will become occupied by the source that is the threat and look for a way to avoid or escape it. There are immediate threats that will make you react suddenly, or there will be threats that will make you plan to be more cautious.

When the system is working the right way, it will prevent you from getting into situations that are dangerous or that can harm you in one way or another.

Types of Fear

Some people have excessive amounts of fear, and these are called phobias. They will have a lot of fear for some stimuli that many people see as not being threatening.

Innate Fear

There are a lot of external factors that are known to make you get afraid, but studies have shown that we are born with some fears. These are termed innate fears. Other fears are called learned.

For instance, those kids that get bullied at school will start fearing to go to school; this is leaned fear.

Innate fear is the one that you are born with – fear of failure, fear of death, and so on. As you grow up, you get to learn about other things that make you become afraid.

Conditioned Fear

Apart from the fears that you get born with, there are other fears that are formed when you come into contact with a negative experience, and you become afraid that something bad will happen again. These fears are usually irrational, and they make us believe that similar circumstances will lead to the same outcome, which is wrong in most instances.

For instance, many people that were attacked by dogs when they were young will cringe at the thought of a dog coming near them. Well, the truth is that a majority of the dogs are very friendly, but just because you had a bad encounter with one, you avoid all of them.

We are also conditioned to fear the things that we are told to be negative. This is why you find so many people and families becoming prejudiced against other people.

How Does Your Brain React to Fear?

When you sense something that makes you become afraid, your body triggers chemicals in your brain that in turn triggers the fear response in the amygdala part of the brain. The amygdala is the first point where the fear response starts from. The amygdala is set up in such a way that it detects the emotional level of stimuli – the extent to which something will affect you.

Let us say you see a lion in the neighborhood, well, the amygdala will respond by triggering the response then will activate all the other areas of the body that are involved in preparing the motor functions that are involved in the response. It also triggers the release of hormones that are responsible for the reaction.

When the response is triggered, bodily changes will get activated, and it will prepare you to react in the right manner. The brain will become alert, the pupils will dilate, and then your breathing accelerates. Blood pressure and heart rate also rise. Since the skeletal muscles are the organs tasked with responding to fear, more flow of blood and glucose will be directed to these muscles. On the other hand, organs that aren't involved in survival, such as the GIT will slow down.

There is a part of the brain called the amygdala that is closely linked to the amygdala. The aim of this part of the brain is to try and interpret the threat that has come up. They will tell you whether the threat that you have experienced is real or not.

Just like any other animals, the many threats of fear that we learn about come from personal experiences that we go through, such as observing other people going through the same experience that we have witnessed. Additionally, we also learn from words, when we are told that something is dangerous, we take this to be the truth, and we react to it the right way.

The good thing about fear is that it makes you focus on something critically. When you are faced with a threat, you tend to be on high alert, and you won't be preoccupied with things that will be on your mind.

Things That You Need to Know About Fear

Feeling afraid doesn't need to be as bad as it should. Before you can look at the various ways to overcome fear, we need to look at a few things about fear itself.

Fear Can Be Healthy

Feeling fear is one of the ways to keep your brain working normally. When you don't show any fear when faced with a threat, people will see that you have a problem with your body system. Reacting to fear makes you human, and it proves to others that you have your emotions in check.

It Comes in Various Intensities

Fear is an unpleasant experience that ranges from mild to highly intense – to a level that it can be paralyzing. Mild news can be from waiting for the results of a test that you have done, and intense fear can be news about an accident that involved someone close to you.

Some intense fear can remain inked on your brain and will require the help of a professional. Constant fear; however mid it is will lead to serious harm to your mental and physical health with time.

It Isn't Automatic

Fear comes from part learned, part instinct, and partly taught. Some of the fears are innate, meaning that they come from your innermost being and you are born with them. The fear of pain is all about survival. The instinct to survive is all about fearing that when you feel the pain, you might end up dying or getting debilitated.

Other types of fear are learned. This means that you get to learn with time to be afraid of certain places and people. When you were born, you never knew that the places existed, but with the time you learned that they aren't the best places to go to.

Some fears are taught. For instance, your culture tells you that some people need to be feared, and others not be feared. Some animals are meant to be feared while others revered.

You Don't Need to Be in A Dangerous Situation to Experience Fear

At times, you don't have to be in the presence of a physical threat to experience fear. Fear can be partly due to your thoughts, and since you have been told s many stories about something, you end up relating it to something else that might be nonexistent.

At times, we experience fear due to our imaginations that lead us into thinking of what could happen.

We are most fearful because of the ability that we have to think, learn, and come up with fear in our minds. At times the fear turns into chronic anxiety that arises from nothing at all.

Fear Dictates What You Do Next

When you experience fear, you will freeze, run, fight, or just get frightened.

Freezing means you stop all that you are doing and focus on the threat so that you decide what to do next. For instance, when you get a message that people will be laid off in the company that you work in.

When you evaluate the situation, the next thing is for you to fight or run. If the threat is manageable, you can decide to handle it heads on, but when the fear is too overwhelming, then you will decide to run.

At times, you neither fight nor flee, you just experience the emotion of fear, and then you take no action at all. However, maintaining a constant state of fright makes you depressed.

How Fear affects the Way You Function

Well, the main aim of fear as an emotion is to help you to avoid dangerous situations. And just because most of the things that we are afraid of today aren't so life-threatening, the response of the body does a lot of harm than good. Let us look at how these emotions affect the way we behave eventually.

Flight or Fight

We have seen the different ways your body responds to threats in the previous paragraphs, and we don't need to repeat them here. All we need to do is to emphasize the fact that your body reacts to threats in various ways to make sure you get away from the threat as fast as possible.

Failure to Make Rational Decisions

When your stress levels rise due to the fear that you experience, you will realize that the body diverts most of its energy to the limbs, and when you are afraid you fail to make rational decisions.

When you experience fear, your brain doesn't turn on the risk-taking functions that are necessary for you to make rational decisions. What happens next is that you won't be able to assess all the options before you make a decision.

This is the reason why you shouldn't force anyone to take big decisions when they are in a situation where they are afraid. They won't be able to think of their options at all.

Everything Turns Negative

When you are faced with a threat, the brain perceives anything and everything around you to be negative. You will associate the buildings, environment, and anything else that is within the vicinity to be negative even if they aren't.

How to Conquer Your Fear

When you keep on ignoring your fear, it grows to chronic proportions. When you decide to face it, it will shrink.

Every start of the year, people come up with resolutions which are goals that they desire to achieve during the year. Many of them fail while others make it. For those that fail, the main reason is that they fear that they won't make it. This prevents them from achieving what they are after, even if they have the capability to succeed.

Here are ways to overcome the fear that you have.

Understand Fear then Embrace It

Fear is there to keep us safe so that we avoid harm. Well, fear cannot be inherently good or bad, but it serves as a tool for us to be able to make decisions.

Fear has its good and bad sides as well, so make sure that you take advantage of the good side and you learn from the bad effects of fear. You can embrace fear so that it helps you to learn lessons but don't let out to control what you do.

Don't Be in a Hurry

When you are faced with a threat, you need to have a plan in mind on how to deal with it. Don't just stand there and wait for something to happen, rather you need to come up with a plan and explore your options.

One of the things that you need to do is to understand what you have at hand to use against the perceived threat. Many undertakings have been ruined because the person failed to make a decision based on what they had at hand. When fear strikes, you take time to consider whether the right action is to jump to the nearest decision or to analyze the various options and make the right decision.

Identify the Fear

At times when you are faced with a threat, try, and understand what kind of fear you are experiencing. Sometimes the mere act of stating what the fear is and then giving it a name will give you the strength you need to deal with it.

Give the fear a name, then give it a size. The size is just the intensity, and it tells you how extensive the fear is so that you can decide whether you can handle it or not. The bigger the fear, the harder it will be for you to handle it.

Remember when you try to ignore fear, it grows to unmanageable proportions, but when you decide to face the fear, it will become smaller.

Think Long Term

If you are a worker, you might think that you won't be available next month in the same position. This is too short a time to start worrying about issues; at times, you need to focus your brain on long term solutions so that you reduce the fear of the unknown.

When you think about a long-term goal, you won't be able to fix the short-term issues, but it will allow you to think about stuff on a more objective scale and come up with the perfect solution.

Educate Yourself

No one is as afraid of anything more than what they don't know. If your fear comes by due to lack of information, then this is the right time to get the information you want so that you get the fear out of the picture.

Take time to understand what the fear is all about then go ahead to know how you can handle it the right way. There are various ways to get this information, including online blogs, research papers, books, and more.

Be Prepared

When you had a negative experience with something, and you failed to handle it the right way, you need to get prepared so that next time you won't have to react negatively again.

Many people have the innate fear of standing in front of people and saying something. So, if you have a fear that is related to your performance in a certain aspect, then you need to prepare for the task well in advance before you face the fear again.

Utilize the Push of Peer Pressure

If you have had a phobia for some time, it is usually good to have a few friends around to help you overcome it.

Have you ever done something that is scary like parachuting out of a moving plane just because you had your friends there to push you to do it?

Peer pressure can be good or bad; it only depends on how the pressure is used. Make sure you surround yourself with people that will help you to overcome fears that are making you fail to make it in life.

Visualize Success

Many people fall into the traps that fear lays because they have a negative mindset that tells them that they will fail. This is especially due to the fear of failure that comes up whenever someone wants to do something.

If you have seen athletes, you will realize that they do their thing with one goal in mind – success.

When they make it mental, they push forward, and then they end up succeeding at what they do.

You also need to adopt this mindset – success, at all times so that you will be prepared to succeed at whatever you try to achieve.

Gain a Sense of Proportion

You need to quantify your fear. For instance, you need to understand how big the threat is that it makes you run wild with fear. At times we get so caught up in the fear that comes with a certain threat that we fail to understand that it is manageable. So, when you are faced with a threat, try, and put a sense of proportion to it before you handle it.

Get Some Help

When you feel like the threat is becoming too chronic and you don't have something to do about it alone, it is time for you to get some help. You can approach a professional therapist to help you overcome your fear or go for friends and colleagues that will help you get over the fear.

If you can't find any of these, then look around for a support group of the issue to assist you. Don't worry if the friends that you work with don't have any experience with the issue at hand – all you need is someone that will guide you the right way.

When you are struggling with your fear, there is someone out there who has the solution that you are really looking for.

Are you doing something which has never been done before and you need to get some guidance on the same? Well, many people have a fear of failure when they go into unchartered waters.

If you are attempting something for the first time, then you need to know that there are some people that have done it before successfully. Is there a formula that they used to succeed? Is there someone that has written a book on the same, or can you use a formula from another area to meet their needs?

Have a Positive Attitude

You need to handle your fear of doing some things by having a positive attitude in all that you do. When you have a positive attitude, things get good and easy. It takes time to develop a positive attitude, but you will be able to get ahead in all that you do better when you have a positive attitude backing you up.

Chapter 7: Emotional Intelligence

Emotional intelligence is the capacity to monitor your emotions as well as to be able to handle the emotions of other people. For you to be emotionally intelligent, you need to be able to distinguish between the different emotions then label them the correct way. Once you do this, the next step is to use the information that you have gathered to guide your behavior and to think as well as to influence the behavior of other people.

Emotional intelligence is whatever we use when we put ourselves in the shoes of other people, have deeper conversations with our spouses or manage a child that is unruly. It allows us to understand ourselves better, connect well with others, and live a happy life that is full of good decisions.

Components of Emotional Intelligence

Before we can look into anything else, it is vital that we understand the components of emotional intelligence. As a person, I have gained a lot of insight into emotional intelligence after I mastered the components of emotional intelligence.

Let us look at these components because they also form the skills that will allow you to interact better with one another.

Self-Awareness

Self-awareness has smaller components that make it one of the best components of emotional intelligence. First, emotional awareness means you get to recognize another person's emotions and its impact on the environment. Additionally, you need to have accurate self-assessment so that you know your limits and strengths. You also need to have self-confidence, which is the ability to be sure of one's capabilities and self-worth.

Self-Regulation

Self-regulation is all about being able to manage your emotions and how they affect you. For you to manage your emotions the right way, you need to maintain high levels of integrity and honesty, as well as take full responsibility for your performance as a person. You also need to be flexible in handling change that comes both professionally and personally.

You also need to be innovative, so that you are comfortable with and open to new information and novel ideas that come your way.

Self-Motivation

As the name suggests, emotional intelligence requires you to have the drive to meet standards. You have to try and improve so that you meet a certain standard of excellence. You also need to be committed to what you do. We are always committed to other things, and we leave what means a lot to us. The commitment that you have needs to be aligned with the goals of the organization and the group. You also need to be ready to grab any opportunities that come your way.

Self-motivation needs a lot of optimism, as well. You need to be persistent when pursuing goals despite the setbacks and obstacles.

Empathy

When you are empathetic, you have the ability to place yourself in another person's situation and understand it. You are able to sense what the other person is going through, and you can see their perspective, and you take an active concern in what they are going through.

As business owners, we are tasked with the responsibility of understanding our customers the right way. When it comes to being empathetic, we are able to recognize, anticipate, and meet our customers' needs the right way.

Empathy doesn't stop at knowing what other people are going through and understanding them; rather, it also begs us to sense what other people need so that we can develop and improve their abilities. To do this, we need to understand what diversity is all about then cultivate the various opportunities through the people that we meet.

Social Skills

Social skills beg us to have influence, which refers to the use of effective tactics to be persuasive all the time. We also need to be able to communicate clearly and in a convincing way. It also encompasses leadership, being agents of change, and being able to manage conflict the right way. We also get to build bonds and collaborate with other people.

The Dimensions of Emotional Intelligence

According to the theorists Mayer and Salovey, there are four unique branches of emotional intelligence that guide us in knowing or emotional abilities and skills. These include:

Perceiving Emotion

Perceiving emotions is all about being able to identify and label the emotions that you come from other people. For instance, if I am in the office, and I call someone that needs to get disciplined, I need to read their emotions so that I understand what they are going through. At times you have to look beyond the mistakes an read the emotions of someone before you get to know what to do.

You also need to express your own emotions the right way. When you express the emotions, you will be able to label them then distinguish between the ones that are honest and dishonest.

Utilize the Emotions

Once you perceive the various emotions, the next step is for you to use them in making decisions. Most of the times, we fail to utilize emotions because we don't know that they are vital to our survival. Instead, we experience them; identify them, and that is that.

For you to utilize emotions, you need to prioritize your thoughts based on the emotions that are associated with different thoughts. You have to learn about and come up with thoughts that will allow you to make better judgments later on. You also need to capitalize on the mood changes so that you appreciate the different points of view, and then use the different emotional states so that you can make better decisions when faced with problems.

Understanding Emotions

You also need to understand emotions the right way. To do this, you need to make sure you identify the emotions the right way then sees the connection between all the emotions. You also have to look at the various causes and consequences of the emotions and then understand the complexity that surrounds them. You also need to look at how the various emotions change from one state to another.

Managing Emotions

This is the final dimension of emotional intelligence. Here, you have to manage both the pleasant as well as the unpleasant emotions, as well as to monitor them then reflecting on them. You need to understand how to prolong your attachment or detach yourself from the emotional state and learn to manage your emotions both within you and in other people.

Examples of Emotional Intelligence in Daily Life

For you to understand what emotional intelligence entails, let us look at the different examples of emotional intelligence in your daily life:

Managing Your Emotions

Say you are deep in a conversation with someone then it suddenly turns from friendly banter into an argument. As you realize that the situation has gone from being a smooth talk to being emotionally charged, you try to work hard to bring the situation under control by controlling the way you react to the situation. You can decide to pull back and reduce on the talk, or you can take leave so that you prevent yourself from saying something that will make you regret.

Managing Other People's Emotions

Once you take your leave, you realize that the other person is still talking about what happened more than necessary. You realize that the person is in an emotional state that makes them furious even when you are calm.

The next step is for you to try and diffuse the situation the right way. You can make efforts to defuse the situation by calling in a few mutual friends to handle the situation or try to change the subject.

If it is necessary that you have to see the conversation till the end, the only logical thing for you to do is to set aside then wait till the person cools down before you can start the subject again. Some people need time to reduce their anger, and this is why you need to allow them enough time to change their frame of mind.

Why You Need to Improve Your Emotional Intelligence

When you hear about emotional intelligence, you need to have a high level, which is why you need to improve on it. Before we look at the various ways of improving your emotional intelligence, we need to look at the various benefits.

It Creates Better Team Work

Teams that have emotionally intelligent members form a good working relationship because they are able to understand each other. They also have good communication and value what every team member contributes to the group. Whenever someone makes a suggestion in the group, all the members get to respond in a productive and positive way.

You Are Able to Deal with Change

Many people don't like change, and they struggle so much to make sure they don't change their beliefs or the way they do things. The good thing is that if you become emotionally intelligent, you get the tools that will help you to deal with the change that comes your way both in personal life and at the workplace.

Others don't resist change, but they regard it with negativity and fail to handle it the right way. When you are emotionally intelligent, you have the capacity to be more positive, and you can inspire your team members to feel that they can accept change.

You Handle Tough Conversations

Whether you are dealing with an angry employee or a customer that is shouting at the top of their voice, difficult conversations usually give rise to a host of emotions. With the right skills, you have the ability to handle the conversations in an emotional way because you can connect with the other person. When you connect with others, you get to find a resolution to issues faster than ever.

Maintaining a conversation, especially in the face of conflict, needs you to have a high level of emotional intelligence. Conflict resolution usually relies on one of the people in the conversation being more intelligent than the other person.

Another benefit of being emotionally intelligent is that you make decisions much better than before. You won't have to base on your own side of the judgment when making a decision; rather, you will be able to struggle less when looking for both sides of the argument.

Helps You to Connect

If you are poor at meeting and talking to people, the most essential ingredient of making things work for you is to be emotionally intelligent. When you are emotionally intelligent, you have the capacity to build trust with other people. Making rapport is also easy and fast. When you meet someone for the first time, you are able to understand what they feel, and you empathize with them to a greater level. This makes you a good part of any team.

Reduce Your Judgment of Other People

As humans, we tend to judge people the moment we see them. This practice starts early in childhood and goes on into our adult years. If you were emotionally intelligent, you wouldn't judge people so much and so quickly. Rather you will try to understand their perspective and then try to understand their perspective, their situation wisely before you jump into conclusions.

Using Emotional Intelligence at the Workplace

As a Leader

While you might not get the chance to interact with everyone in the workplace, the attitude of the company starts with you. If you desire to have an engaged employee, it is vital that you show them by example.

Leaders also need to know that they are following a chain of command in the office, and they need to make sure the chain moves down the right way. Leaders need to make sure that their behavior has a positive impact on the people that are around them. Try and make every employee feel important in all that they do.

Heading a Meeting

When you are the head of the meeting, you need to make sure you understand the prevailing mood in the room before you make any decision. You need to be able to identify and read the body language of the people that are in attendance and observe whether they are comfortable or scared. Using emotional intelligence, you have the power to read what the people think so that you talk to them the right way.

While it is good for you to have a lively discussion while at it, the leader needs to make sure that every attendee gets the opportunity to speak and get heard.

Attending a Meeting

The person chairing the meeting isn't the only one that should be worried about using emotional intelligence while they are in the room. It is important for you as the attendee as well to understand what is happening.

Try to speak during the meeting so that people can hear your opinion. When you contribute to discussions, you will get to be considered for future discussions later on.

If you are a shy employee, you need to step out of your comfort zone and recognize the situation that needs you to speak up.

Additionally, when you decide to talk in a meeting, you need to welcome any suggestions that come your way and try to consider others even if they seem to be less helpful. Instead of focusing on a negative comment from the boss, it is better to use it to change the way you behave in the workplace.

After Receiving Feedback

For many people, using emotional intelligence doesn't stop the moment the meeting gets finished. Rather, you also have to respond to the type of feedback that you receive from the meeting. One of the tenets of using emotional intelligence is when you have to adapt to various aspects of the meeting, such as receiving feedback.

During Networking Events

Networking events can be rather intimidating for people that are shy and introverted, but they form some of the most important opportunities for professionals that want to enhance their careers. Emotional intelligence is very important during these events as it allows introverts to get out of their comfort zones and interact with other people despite their discomfort.

As an extrovert, you need to use the various instances to make sure the conversation isn't one-sided, but rather two-sided. You also need to tone down and allow introverts to approach you when they feel comfortable to do it.

As a Hiring Manager

The most proactive time that you need to use emotional intelligence at work is when you need to hire a new employee. You need to get the right person to help you achieve the goals of the organization.

When you meet with the potential employee, you need to learn to read their mind and then know when to ask a question and when to respond to their queries. If you ask a question and the candidate struggles to find an

When looking for the perfect employee, you need to be careful so that you hire someone that is competent and has high emotional intelligence.

How to Improve Your Emotional Intelligence

In any competitive environment, you need to develop your emotional intelligence so that you succeed at what you do. Let us look at the top ways of increasing your emotional intelligence:

1. ***Learn to Respond instead of Reacting***

    When faced with a situation that threatens to become conflicting, you need to learn to respond rather than reacting to the conflict. When faced with a conflict, feelings of anger, as well as high levels of emotions, are too common. They push you to make impulsive decisions which will lead to bigger problems as well.

You need to understand that when faced with conflict, the solution you are looking for is a resolution to that conflict and nothing else.

You also ought to understand that conflict resolution is all about the two of you – when you fail to see sense in the argument, you will not see an end to the conflict.

2. *Learn to Listen*

Many conversations go south because one of the people that are involved in the conversation fails to listen to what the other person is saying.

Emotionally intelligent people have mastered the art of listening, and they wait for their turn before they speak. They make sure that they listen and then understand what is being said before they respond.

They also listen to the body language of the conversation, making sure that they read the various facial expressions, the gestures and body movements of the person before they make any assumptions.

When you learn to listen, you prevent any misunderstandings that might come up, and you also learn to respond the right way and show respect to the person you are speaking to.

3. *Maintain a Positive Attitude*

Anytime you approach someone with a negative attitude; you will not listen at all to what they have to say. This is because you have already made a judgment in your mind that the person is wrong or that they aren't up to par, and this will become a stumbling block when it comes to an understanding of them.

Emotionally intelligent people have learned how to be aware of those around them, and they reserve their attitude so that they don't let anything slip. They know what they need to do so that they can have a good day and enjoy an optimistic outlook toward other people.

4. *Take Criticisms Well*

A vital part of increasing your emotional intelligence is to tale criticisms well. Instead of always getting defensive or offended for small things, you need to take some time to understand where the criticism is coming from and then how it affects other people or their performance. They then take some time to resolve any issues that come up in a constructive manner.

5. *They Empathize*

People that are emotionally intelligent have the capacity to empathize with others. They know that empathy shows that they are strong, not weak. When you are empathetic, you get to relate to other people at a basic human level, and it opens a lot of doors for mutual respect and understanding between people that have differing opinions.

Chapter 8: Your Attitude

You r attitude defines anything and everything that happens in your life. Have you seen those people that have the energy of a 20-year-old but the looks of a 40-year-old? Such people are endearing to every person that they meet, and they make it easy.

You will also come across a person that doesn't have the capacity to draw attention to them. They aren't happy and are always negative in everything that they do.

All this has to do with attitude.

The attitude that you adopt has a huge bearing on what you do with your lives. It influences how you see and interact with the world around you.

When you have a good attitude, your life will be full of happiness. As you know too well, good things happen to good people, and when you have a great attitude, then great things will happen to you as well. Negative attitudes turn into negative actions, and these result in negative results.

When you make that decision about your everyday attitude, you get to define the happiness in your lives. You will be able to define the quality of your life by just having the right attitude.

Attitude for People Close to You

Friends

Friends have a special place in our lives, and this is because they listen to us, encourage us, and support us. Well, this is what you need to expect from your friends.

The quality of friends that you have depends a lot on your attitude. When you have a certain attitude, you get to attract a certain type of people to be your friends based on the attitude. If you have a positive attitude, you will attract friends that are positive, and if you have a negative attitude, you will attract friends who are negative.

For instance, previously, I had a negative outlook and low self-esteem, and I found it so hard to connect to people to have good relationships with them. When I discovered that the major problem as my attitude, I decided to change it and fast-forward a few years now, I am happy because I changed my attitude towards life. I did away with negative friends, and currently, I have a close group of friends. All the friends I have are armed with a great attitude, and I spend a lot of time with them.

Lover

Just the way it influences friendship, attitude also defines the people that you love. A positive attitude will make sure you attract a person that is suitable for your life. When you have a positive attitude, you get to build a relationship that is based on fun, passion, love, and happiness. A negative attitude, on the other hand, will build a relationship that is full of anger, mistrust, depression, and resentment.

As an example, before I met Carol, I had endured a lot of negative relationships that didn't do anything for me. I had been manipulated, cheated on, and even taken for granted. Well, the relationships had some great times, but overall, I would say that my past relationships had been awful. Then I decided to change my attitude, and then things started falling in place by themselves. I was able to love myself rather than focusing all my energies on people that weren't grateful. I started believing that I deserved something better, and that is exactly what I ended up with.

Work

When you join a company or any other place that you provide your services, your attitude matters a lot. Many people out there don't enjoy what they do; this is because they don't follow their passion; rather, they work just to pay their bills and then get on in life.

Instead of turning up to work when they are overjoyed, they turn up when they are already annoyed and looking for someone that they can take out their stress upon.

Early on in my life, I used to be at a position where I hated the work that I did. I never appreciated what I went through each day, and it made me lose syke each and every day. The work was a lot and boring, to say the least, and I saw that everyone else was incompetent and had a negative attitude. The bosses didn't do anything to help the situation. Then I changed my attitude, I decided to look at the job in a positive light, and this made a lot of difference in my life.

Where Do Our Attitudes Come From?

Studies show that approximately 90 percent of our attitudes come from our childhoods. The first words that we learn when we are born are daddy, mommy, and no. We get to have a lot of no's in our early lives that when we get to our teens, we have turned the no's into impossibilities.

As we move into adulthood, we believe that the no's become fears, and we can't do anything because we have grown up knowing that it doesn't work at all.

Types of Attitudes

In life, we have different attitudes that define your position in life. We shall not look at the positive or negative attitudes at this juncture; rather, we want to look at what point are you in life. Here is a lowdown on what to expect at any point in time:

The Poverty Attitude

This is an attitude of the people that are generally afraid and don't look for any opportunity that might help them generate any income for their livelihood.

Such people usually blame others for the failures in their lives, and they feel that they have a right to enjoy what happens for them without paying a single cent. This type of attitude usually encourages a sense of dependence, whereby the person feels that other people owe them something.

People that have this attitude usually have little or no money and will force you to pay their bills citing lack of money.

Paycheck to Paycheck

This attitude is a step right above the poverty attitude. This person is looking for a job just to pay bills and will take very few risks. They don't focus so much on the reward; rather, they put their whole mind on the risk that they are up against.

Such people become bitter towards their friends who are successful, and they go through a lot of fear because they are in their comfort zone at all times. They have a lot of hate towards anything that might compromise their salary or wages.

The Middle Income Attitude

This is a somewhat healthy attitude, and such people will spend their time on get-rich-quick schemes that will make them no money at all at the end of it all. These people generally have a lot of time and think that when they gamble with their money, they will make a lot more only to lose it.

They usually have a lot of time on their hands and are usually open to training and coaching to improve their position.

The Game Player

This is the middle-income level that can do well with coaching. The person will take another person's game then they will take it to the highest level. They are good at making things work for them, and they don't accept staying down at any time.

The Game Maker

This person creates his or her own opportunity and makes a lot from it. They usually create a lot of wealth, and they see themselves as a partner in the chosen product or a company. They are usually concerned about the success of a company as well as their own success, and they come with a lot of confidence and make a lot of money.

These are just a few attitudes that tell you where you are in life. Let us look at the benefits of having a positive attitude.

How to Improve on Your Attitude in life

When you are faced with any situation, a positive attitude is all you need to take yourself to the next level. Let us look at ways to improve your attitude:

Appreciate

Everyone has that circumstance in life that takes a toll on them each day. Many times, we let negative circumstances to get the best of us, and this is why we find that the mental attitude takes a huge beating.

When you are faced with a tough circumstance, you need to reflect on what has happened before and how well it was. Try and focus on the positive side of things and be grateful for what you have achieved so far.

Think about your life, and think about the people that haven't made it to that point. Even the simplest things such as your job and your family need to make you smile and be in good moods. Each of these things, however simple, are a true blessing, and you need to make sure that you feel them in your life.

Not everyone is healthy – some are in hospital, and others are dead – be thankful for these and more.

Have Faith

Studies show that more than 90 [percent of all the things that people worry about don't happen. The remaining 10 percent is way beyond your control, and so you don't have anything to do about them at all – they just happen naturally.

You need to believe in something so that you can move ahead. First, you need to try and have faith in yourself, knowing that you will handle things the way they come. When you believe in yourself, you get the chance to push ahead and the determination to make things work.

Guard Your Mind

Your mind is the best resource you have. When you do anything, make sure you look at the various influences in your life then decide which ones need to be eliminated and which ones need to be minimized.

Find things that will make you work better rather than work harder. Try and associate with people that will help you grow rather than the ones that will have a negative influence on your attitude. Avoid people that will constantly try to take you down, and instead, look for people that will help you grow your career or be a better person.

Feed the Mind

Your mind is like your body – when you feed it, the more it becomes active. Try and read motivational and inspirational literature that will encourage you. If you don't have any time for reading, you can download audio files that will help you become a better person.

Music has a huge impact on how you think and act. Make sure you select the right type of music that will allow you to think positive thoughts.

You also need to seek conversations with people that are positively minded. If you realize that a conversation that you are having has taken a negative turn, exit the conversation, or interject with the aim of changing the subject.

Change Your Speech

Words have a lot of power behind them. If you profess to yourself that you are a loser, then you will find that you become one. Try to choose your words carefully, both that you tell yourself and those that you say to other people. Words can be used to tear down or to build others. Remember that what you tell someone influences what they see when they look at you.

When you talk, the words are originating from your mind, which means that your words are a reflection of your thoughts and your ideas. Try to change your speech, and you will see your attitude change as well.

When you change your words, you also change the relationship you have with others, but most importantly, you get to change what is within yourself.

Lighten Up

Whenever possible, begin by being friendly to other people. Try and lighten up when you meet strangers, so that you are someone that people want to be around with. Remember that people tend to like people that are easy to interact with rather than those that are hard to talk to.

Chapter 9: Goals in Life

Are you out to enjoy unmetered success? I am guessing you are since you are reading this section. Goals are all about putting into perspective what you desire to achieve in the future then going after them.

Have you ever asked yourself what makes you succeed and another person struggle? It is because they have the capacity to set goals and then go after the goals with determination.

Image: the structure of our goals

Let us first look at the types of goals that you can have that will help you grow before we look at the benefits of goal setting and how to set the perfect goals.

Types of Goals

Goals can be categorized in different ways, depending on what you want to achieve. You can set goals for business, education, personal life, or your career. Let us look at these types.

Educational Goals

For you to grow and see a change in your life, first you need to learn. Learning is all about getting information into your system that you didn't have before. Education isn't just about a school – it transcends into vocational studies, university, and even professional qualifications.

These goals won't remain the same throughout – they will change as you move from one state to another. The goals that you had in education ten years ago might not be the same goals you have at the moment.

You need to remember that education doesn't stop. It is always lifelong, and you need to try and expand your brain in various different ways.

As you progress, the goals in education change according to the career path that you have decided upon. You might decide to retrain your mind in a whole new area when you get the ability.

Relationship Goals

While we might be complete in all that we do, we need to have people in our lives to play that huge role that we need – to feel loved and appreciated. Relationship goals allow you to find something that can enhance your life as well as benefit other people. The better you become at achieving them will deeply impact the people around you as well as your personal happiness.

For you to achieve these goals, you need to have enough time on your hand and for your family as well as your friends.

Physical Goals

Our bodies, physical abilities, and health have a huge influence on the lives that we lead and what we are able to achieve. The goals that you set in this area depend so much on your age and the state of health that you are currently in.

If you are still young and fit, then the goals you set will be likely the ones to push yourself a little bit further such as a marathon.

On the other hand, if you are middle-aged and you sit behind the desk all day long, then you will try to keep the goals within normal ranges for your age.

Personal Development Goals

The only constant we have in life is change, and this goes for every person – young and old. Depending on what we value most, we have the ability to develop in so many ways.

If you feel the need to stretch yourself mentally and physically by doing something, it all depends on you. You can decide to learn salsa, go to the gym, or master a new technique.

The need to develop personal goals is just that – you need to look at the way things are going in your life then you decide to change something.

For personal development to work, the drive to succeed needs to come from deep within. You can broaden your mind by reading or traveling the world, learning new skills, and going for self-improvement.

Financial Goals

Money will determine how everything works in your life – even relationships. This is why it is one of the most popular areas that you need to look at when it comes to setting goals and achieving them. No matter the career that you are in, one of your inspirations is to make money.

If you have been unfortunate enough to get into debt, you will set a goal for having a budget the next time you decide to spend money. You also need to adjust your spending habits so that you do things the right way.

Another goal that many people like making is building their own house. Although it requires careful thought, it will help if you decide to build a house the right way.

Another common financial goal is retirement. You need to take careful thought to decide when to retire because you know then you won't have a salary coming in every month.

Career Goals

We spend a lot of our lives working, which is why you need to have a goal in mind when you do so.

Career goals are connected to education because you cannot have a career without some education. So, you need to make an effort to study and then improve your skillset so that you open up new career avenues for your life.

Many people have a few ideas of what they are looking for in terms of their career. You might aim to get a particular accolade, start your own business, or build on your earning power.

When you start your career, you need to come up with a list of career goals that will form the basis of a master plan that will dictate your career development. This forms the first step towards your future.

Spiritual Goals

For those that are religious, spiritual goals are another area that is connected with other parts of your life. These include personal development as well as relationships.

Whether you follow a certain religious faith or not, when you develop your spiritual self, you underpin nearly everything that you do.

You can set yourself some time to do voluntary work or donate more money to the less fortunate. Maybe you desire to work as a missionary for some time before you get back to your home.

Either way, you need to make sure that the religious goals that you come up with don't affect the people that are around you.

Goals According to Time

Goals can also be long term or short term, depending on the time that you allocate them.

Long term goals are the plans that you make for the future - they are the ones that will take more than a year typically down the road. Long term goals are usually achieved over time as a person completes the various stages of their life.

People set long term goals because they envision what they want to do and where they want to be in, say, five to 20 years from the current time.

Examples of long-term goals include;

- Get your master's degree
- Buy a bigger house
- Retire
- Own your own company
- Run and complete a marathon

On the other hand, short term goals are the ones that you will achieve in the near future, usually in less than a year. They are usually stepping stones to achieve long-term goals. You need to see long term goals as a series of short-term goals that take you to the ultimate goal that you have.

Examples of short-term goals include:

- Join a gym
- Lose a few pounds
- Start yoga
- Get a distinction in class
- Get a job during the summer
- Build a gazebo

Lifetime goals, on the other hand, are the major goals that you wish to accomplish in a lifetime. These goals can be accomplished later in life. These have accomplishment dates of ten years or more in the future. Examples include getting a job as a teacher, graduating from college, or buying a house.

Lifetime goals are usually general at first, but when you start working towards them, they start to become more specific. They are usually those meaningful and vital goals that you come up with. The only issue is that achieving the goals is usually far in the future. This way, you might find that you have trouble being focused on the goals.

How to Set the Right Goals

Believe

Before you can start setting goals, you need to believe in the process of setting goals. If you don't believe that you can transform your life to get what you want, then you can as well forget about setting goals and go-ahead to do something else.

If you are in doubt, take a look around you, and you will realize that the start of anything is a thought. The thought then is transformed into something else, such as a blueprint.

Visualize

After you have a belief in something, the next step is for you to visualize what you desire to happen. If you need to have a company a year from now, you need to visualize the different changes that need to take place before you can come up with the blueprint.

The clearer you visualize, the better the ability to make it happen.

Write it down

Jotting down the dream is a key goal of success. When you write the goals down, you become a creator. Failure to write these goals down will often mean that you won't forget or you won't focus on them. Make sure you write the goals down at a place that you can see each day.

Have a Purpose

The need to achieve the goal should drive you to make changes in your life. You need to know why you should achieve the goals in the first place because it will direct you to your destination.

Knowing why you need something so bad will give you a strong motivation to see it through to the finish line.

Commit Yourself to The Process

This might seem to be such an obvious process, but it comes with negative consequences if you take it lightly. You need to make sure you commit yourself to the process of making sure you achieve each goal. Know why the goals are important to you and then focus on making sure you get the outcome right.

When you commit to the goal, you also need to focus on the results. If you get distracted, you will notice that you end up running after goals that have no role in your ultimate results.

The good thing is that without regular practice, you will be easily distracted.

Have a Plan

If you wish to achieve your goals, you need to have a plan of action that is clear. Write the goals down and make sure you have them in steps so that you know your progress. When you have a plan of action, you will have the chance to edit it when things go wrong or when they aren't working as you had planned.

Be Accountable

For you to push through when things start getting tough, you need to make sure you hold yourself accountable for what happens. Unless you have a coach that will do things for you, it is vital that you have to hold yourself accountable in all ways.

For you to stay accountable, try sharing your goals with people that are close to you.

Run a Review

You need to make it a part of the day to review the progress of your goals each time. When you review your goals each time, you will keep them alive in your mind, and you will convert them into actionable steps.

When you review your goals, you will stay aware of them, and you will not feel stuck when one doesn't work out because you will compensate it somewhere else.

Chapter 10: Brain Detox Formula

Detoxification has become the hype these days, and you will hear it being thrown right left and center all over the internet and other places. So, what's detoxification?

According to physiology, detoxification is a function of the cells. When your body detoxifies, it collects all the debris in the form of toxins and debris, and then it pushes them out of the body. We remove the toxins from the body using different mechanisms, including the GIT, GUT, respiratory tract, sweat glands, and other channels.

The brain is made up of cells, and these cells detoxify themselves just like the rest of your body, removing toxins so that the brain can stay healthy. There are various ways for you to encourage the detoxification process of the brain, which will keep its decline at bay.

Let us look at the various ways you can do this.

From Self to Social Awareness

When you have good social awareness, you will be able to understand and read situations accurately because you are able to empathize with their emotions at all times.

Social awareness allows you to understand and then respond to the needs of other people. Many people are self-aware, which makes them unable to read the mood of others. When you are socially aware of other people, you need to have empathy, organizational awareness, and service.

Empathy refers to the ability to understand the emotions of other people, their needs, as well as their concerns. While organizational awareness is the ability to understands the things that happen in the organization and how they affect the workers. Service, on the other hand, looks at the ability to understand and meet the needs of your customers.

Being aware of social situations means that you get to consider carefully all that the people want then plan to communicate to them in a way that will meet their needs.

The good thing about social awareness is that it is part of you – a natural response to what happens to us when we meet new people.

To make your brain to detox, you need to be active, and one of the best ways to do this is to become socially aware.

Self-Reflecting and Mindfulness

Mindfulness comes with very many positive impacts on your life and the lives of other people. Just by undertaking a mindfulness practice, you will be able to start to see life shift in ways that you have never imagined before. When you start to establish a mindfulness practice, there are a few things that you can do so that you improve it.

One of the best ways to improve your mindfulness is via self-reflection. Self-reflection is the act of examining your own self so that you can grow, get in touch with your feelings, and then create a better self-image in your life.

When you use self-reflection, you will be able to get a clearer image of the point where you are in life and how you feel in any situation. With this information, you can make better decisions and understand how to make your daily life better.

When you become mindful through self-reflection, you get to develop yourself both on a personal as well as a professional level. Through the act of self-evaluation, you will know where you are in life. You get to answer a lot of questions that include the point where you are in your personal situation, how do you feel about it, what is your personal situation, are you happy with your chosen profession and whether you desire to make changes in your field of work in a certain way.

As you ask the questions, and you become aware of your current situation, you will be more aware of yourself and how you feel.

Mindfulness and self-reflection help you to improve your relationships in the right way. This doesn't apply only to your external relationships but your inner self as well. When you examine yourself, and you find that you aren't treating yourself or other people the way you would like, you need to try and change your actions, conversations, and self-talk.

Mindfulness also allows you to get in touch with the present moment and then to enjoy all that it has to offer you. When you get in touch with your inner self, you will become more aware of how you feel, think, and act.

For you to understand yourself and reflect upon it, you need to be aware of the present and then take time to appreciate, feel, and reflect on it. Start by asking yourself a few questions that tell you how you feel and then recognize your current physical and emotional state.

How to Trigger Change in Your life

If you desire to make a change in your personal life, you need to follow a few tips. First, you have to identify the things that you need to change. You must first understand why you are out to make a change in the first place. Start by identifying the core values in your life, then identify the things that are vital to you.

Identify the things that make you a whole person, then go ahead and look at ways that you can change them.

If you have goals, try, and make sure these goals align with your values, doing this will give you direction.

Another tip is for you to remove any negativity that is in your life. It might sound simple, but it isn't as simple as you might think.

When you are surrounded by negativity, you will not be able to have a joyful and positive life at all.

People that have a negative attitude are ever stressed, get sick all the time, and have fewer opportunities than those that are positive.

You also need to be kind to other people, because when you engage in kindness, you will feel good as a person and you will be more optimistic, moral, and more positive.

There are various ways that you can be kind to other people, and it won't take a lot of time and effort. You can decide to visit the sick or to give to the less fortunate in society. You can also choose to volunteer whenever you feel like it. Kindness can even be in the form of a smile that you give to the people that you meet on the road.

After coming up with the things that are vital in your life, the next step is to eliminate anything else that isn't important. This is aimed at making your life simple so that you can focus on things that are vital in your life.

We usually have a lot of things in our lives that we always feel overloaded at all times. Most of the things that we hold on to aren't that important to us; we need to get rid of them the right way. For instance, if you have a business, try, and eliminate any unneeded expenses so that you reduce the level of stress.

Go for Useful Knowledge

The benefits of access to knowledge are numerous. When you access knowledge the right way, and in the best context, you get to know things that many people don't know, and you also get to understand way better than other people. You also get to make decisions based on facts rather than hearsay.

When you have access to knowledge, you also have a sense of pride and accomplishment that doesn't come easy to many people. When you have the knowledge, you will have the capacity to say that you accomplished something new.

However, for you to gain the knowledge, you have to give up something – your time and attention that you give to others.

With access to knowledge, you get to grow personally, and you can build your knowledge base and improve yourself for the better at all times.

Access to knowledge also gets you access to new and different opportunities as well as the chance to try our new experiences that might turn out to be better than the ones that you have ever tried.

Additionally, when you have knowledge as your forte, you get the chance to earn more money in your life. This is because you will have a new skill that you will have learned that will link to the work that you do. If your working life has been stagnant, you can rejuvenate it and get much more out of it.

Additionally, when you develop a new skill, you get to influence how you do things on a daily basis, and this will make things easier and quicker for you, which in turn saves you time, stress, and energy.

When you learn something new, your brain chemistry will also change. This will improve your performance on various tasks. When you learn and grasp something new, you get to learn better. Additionally, when you learn a new skill, you get to learn things faster over time.

The Power of Active Reach and Visualization

When you decide to run your tasks in an active manner, you will be able to reach out to people actively, and then you can change what you feel and how you do things.

Visualization can help you reach your goals the right way.

In your life as well as your work, you need to know that success always begins with having a goal. If you decide to lose weight or stop smoking, you need to start off with an idea or a thought. Whether big or small, the goals that you come up with always give you a purpose, and they help you do the right thing all the time.

However, you need to know that for you to reach your destination, you need to have a lot of determination and commitment.

The sad thing is that many people get stuck in the goal-setting stage. They start out with good intentions; then they just don't seem to make things happen the right way.

Before you can believe in a goal, you have to visualize it. You need to have an idea of what your goal looks like then go after it. Remember the old adage – seeing believes? Well, it works the way it is phrased out.

This is when visualization comes in – this is a technique that allows you to create a mental image of something that will come in the future. When you visualize an upcoming event, you will see the possibility of achieving it. The visualization shows you what the future holds for you, and it makes you feel motivated and ready to pursue the goal.

Visualization is a method that is developed to improve performance and is supported by facts and scientific evidence to get to where you wish to be.

Visualization works because the brain interprets it as an action that will happen. The brain gets primed in such a way that it creates memories that will force your body to behave the way you imagined. All this occurs without having to perform the activity – but it achieves a similar result somehow.

How to Develop the Ability to Change Your Life

Change is inevitable; in fact, the only constant in life is change. When you are faced with a situation, the only thing that will make things work for you is change. If you don't change, you won't have the capacity to grow as a person.

You won't grow if you can't change the way you think, behave, and do things. The good thing is that the change in your life is a continuous process that will let you grow. When you stop changing, you stop growing.

For you to change, you need to slow down. Slowing down doesn't mean that you stop working and doing things the way they need to be done, rather you need to take some time and reflect on what you are doing.

Now that you have reflected on your life, you need to end up with a few areas that need to change. Note the few areas down so that you are always reminded of what you need to do so that you change. The next step is for you to be willing to change.

You might have everything written down, but if you aren't willing to change, you won't have a chance in life at all. For you to be willing to change, you need first to realize that things can be better if you decide to change some things. No matter how your life is, there are some things that can always be improved. The change that you need in your life is a process that takes time and effort, embrace it.

Revisit, Reinforce and Rehearse

When you do something, you need to be able to monitor how it works for you. When you decide to change your life, you need to take time and first look at where you are and where you want to be. Look at the point that you started out from and then look at where you desire to be. Take time to compare your results and what you have achieved so far.

If the results aren't satisfactory, take time to do things again the best way, and then review your results again. The best thing about making things work for you is that you can repeat, refine your results, and then try again.

Conclusion

Thanks for making it through to the end of the book, let's hope it was informative and able to provide you with all of the tools you need to achieve your goals, whatever it is that they may be. Just because you've finished this book doesn't mean there is nothing left to learn on the topic, and expanding your horizons is the only way to find the mastery you seek.

Now that you have made it to the end of this book, you hopefully have an understanding of how to get started mastering your emotions once and for all, as well as a strategy or two, or three, that you are anxious to try for the first time. Before you go ahead and start giving it your all, however, it is important that you have realistic expectations as to the level of success you should expect in the near future.

While it is perfectly true that some people experience serious success right out of the gate, it is an unfortunate fact of life that they are the exception rather than the rule. What this means is that you should expect to experience something of a learning curve, especially when you are first figuring out what works for you. This is perfectly normal, however, and if you persevere you will come out the other side better because of it. Instead of getting your hopes up to an unrealistic degree, you should think of your time spent improving your emotional control as a marathon rather than a sprint which means that slow and steady will win the race every single time.